How to Have All the Answers When the Questions Keep Changing

Hundreds of Tips, Tricks and Techniques for Thriving In a Changing Workplace

By
Karin Ireland

CAREER PRESS
3 Tice Road, P.O. Box 687
Franklin Lakes, NJ 07417
1-800-CAREER-1; 201-848-0310 (NJ and outside U.S.)
FAX: 201-848-1727

Copyright © 1996 by Karin Ireland

HOW TO HAVE ALL THE ANSWERS WHEN THE QUESTIONS KEEP CHANGING
ISBN 1-56414-250-7, $6.99, Cover design by Dean Johnson Design, Inc.
Printed in the U.S.A. by Book-mart Press

To order this title by mail, please include price as noted above, $2.50 handling per order, and $1.00 for each book ordered. Send to: Career Press, Inc., 3 Tice Road, P.O. Box 687, Franklin Lakes, NJ 07417. Or call toll-free 1-800-CAREER-1 (NJ and Canada: 201-848-0310) to order using VISA or MasterCard, or for further information on books from Career Press.

Library of Congress Cataloging-in-Publication Data

Ireland, Karin.
    How to have all the answers when the questions keep changing:
  hundreds of tips, tricks, and techniques for thriving in a changing
  workplace / by Karin Ireland.
      p. cm.
    ISBN 1-56414-250-7 (pbk.)
    1. Career development. 2. Organizational change. 3. Adaptability
(Psychology) I. Title.
HF5381.I638 1996
650.1--dc20

96-22573
CIP

For Sid Sturgis, with much "aloha."

I'd like to thank my friends in the Patent groups for seeing who I am, listening to my dreams and encouraging me to "go for it!": Irene Borg, Erika Shaw, Dianne Maresh, Tina Hennings, Jerry Hennings, Jo-Ann Andre and Joan Lively. Thanks to Pauline Hardin and Suzi Coy, for offering me links to my new home. And a special thanks to Tricia Ireland, who always believes in me.

Success in the changing workplace

Life as we know it is changing dramatically, especially at work.

What with downsizing, restructuring and reengineering, and technology becoming outdated six months after it's introduced, it's becoming harder and harder to have all the answers. We don't even know what the *questions* will be tomorrow.

It used to seem that the important questions—and their answers—were going to stay the same for years, maybe forever. We knew that if we worked hard, we'd be rewarded with raises and even promotions. We knew what it took to get ahead, and when we didn't know enough, our employers provided us with job training. We knew the financial commitments we could make because our jobs were secure. Employers were willing to provide that security as long as we did a good job.

But today, the question "Will I always work at this job?" has changed to "Will I have a job next month at all?" At a deeper level, what we really want to know is: "Will I be okay?" We're challenged with finding ways to answer yes.

To have all the answers, we need to accept responsibility for our own lives in ways we've never been expected to before. That doesn't necessarily mean doing more—in fact, increasing our pace only contributes to the confusion. Instead, it means doing what we do differently and letting go of old beliefs about how things should be.

Most of us have been taught that the known is safe and the new may be risky. But today, what's risky is *resisting* change.

That can cost you your health because of the stress it causes. It can also cost you your job.

Most of us will spend 10,000 to 12,000 days of our lives at work. That's nearly 32 *years*. Why spend that time feeling uncertain and insecure? Learn how to be happier, more confident and more successful at work, no matter how it changes.

Some of the suggestions in this book may surprise you. A few may seem the opposite of what you thought you needed to do, and that's good. When the questions change, the answers need to change—and so do you.

Find ways to be your own security blanket. Look for ways to be a satisfied and valued employee...

"The purpose of life is to be happy."

—The Dalai Lama

Practice relying more on yourself and less on others. Look for ways to reduce dependency on your job. Pay off debts. Avoid taking on new ones.

Lighten up. Don't take anything—including yourself—so seriously.

❖•◈•❖

Be willing to have fewer absolute opinions. Fewer absolute needs.

❖•◈•❖

Give yourself permission not to know everything. Give yourself permission to try new things and fail.

Success is a feeling—not a job title, a house or a car.

"Believe in yourself, and what others think won't matter."
—Ralph Waldo Emerson,
19th-century American poet

If what you've been doing to solve a problem doesn't work, try something new. Almost anything will be more likely to work than what hasn't so far.

With downsizing, smartsizing and rightsizing (or whatever your employer calls it), it's easy to get so busy doing what has to be done that you forget to do what will move you toward your goals. Being overworked can become a habit. At least once a month, ask yourself:

- What things do you do at home and at work that don't really have to be done?
- What things don't have to be done so often? So well? What doesn't have to be done by *you*?

Write down your new goals. Read the goals you've written down in the past. What steps can you take in the next month to help you reach them?

Ask for what you want. Do you want to work on a specific project? Do you want a window cubicle, an assistant, a raise? Do you want the company to help pay for classes that will improve your job skills? It's not enough to hint and hope someone will offer. You may have been taught that asking for what you want is selfish or pushy, or that you may sound ungrateful. But if you don't ask for what you want at work, you'll get whatever someone else decides to give you. When you want something at work:

- Ask when the time is right, not when you're in the mood.
- Don't hint. Don't be vague. Be specific about what you want and *when*.
- Ask politely and confidently. Don't whine.

- Ask as if you expect to get it—as if you know it's already yours.
- Look for ways that getting what you want will benefit the giver, too. Mention those benefits when you ask.
- Don't give up if you don't get it the first time. Wait and ask again.

When asking for a raise:

- If possible, ask right after successfully completing a major project.
- Find out what the range for your position is, and ask for an amount near, but not over, the top.

- If you're already at the top, ask about having your job reclassified. Remember, though, this may result in additional responsibilities for you.
- Don't expect an answer on the spot, but do ask for an estimate of when you can expect an answer.

Use a journal. Make lists. When thoughts of all the tasks you need to complete are chasing themselves through your head like a classroom of unruly kindergartners, get them out of your mind and onto paper.

To determine if a task is a priority or not, ask:

- Will it affect revenues?
- Is there a legal need for compliance?
- Does it affect customer relations/service?
- Will doing it, or doing it a certain way, matter next year? Next month?

To make good decisions:

- Know what you want to accomplish in the long run. Measure each option against that goal.
- Notice how your body feels when you contemplate each option. Tense? Jittery? Relaxed?

- Make a list of the pros and cons for each option.
- Ask yourself whose messages you're listening to about each option. Your own? A parent's? A sibling's? A spouse's? Begin to listen to your own inner voice more and more.
- Realize that most of today's decisions won't matter 10 years from now.
- Realize that most decisions aren't right or wrong but are simply a choice between one option and another.
- Promise yourself beforehand that you won't beat yourself up if you later believe that you should have made a different decision.
- Assign each option to a side of a coin. Flip the coin and see how you feel about the result. If you don't feel good, do the opposite.

> *"There is nothing either good or bad,*
> *but thinking makes it so."*

—Shakespeare

If you want to advance to the executive level in your company, work toward supervisory positions in departments directly linked to company profits, such as product development or sales, rather than support staff positions in support departments, such as security, communications or the print shop.

Join professional organizations. Don't just show up at the monthly meetings, though—get involved. Serve on committees for experience that could help you advance in your job. Hold a position of high visibility so people will know you when you ask for help finding your next job. Consider other members when you're looking for staff for *your* department. Exchange information you've collected about trends in your field with other members.

If you work from home, rent a box at a commercial mail service and use that address on your business cards. This will look professional and also prevent business contacts from showing up at your home unannounced and uninvited.

Learn basic financial planning. Use credit cards only in cases of emergency. Add to your savings account regularly. Consult a financial investment counselor. Take a finance class at your local college. It's not always how much you earn but what you *do* with what you earn that results in financial security.

Learn how to be a team player. That means you don't get to play all the positions, and you can't take credit for all the wins. But then again, you don't get blamed for all the losses, either.

Develop a reputation for being a valuable worker. Do a little bit more than you absolutely have to do. If you have an idea that will simplify or add value to a project, make the extra effort to do it.

Things a boss looks for in a worker:

- Someone who gets along with other employees.
- Someone who is positive and optimistic.
- Someone who is accurate, reliable and responsible.
- Someone who offers solutions instead of complaints.
- Someone who is loyal.

Always check—and double-check—your facts.

Get what you're supposed to get done before you do tasks you think are more interesting.

Every day, look for new ways to increase your opinion of yourself. Spend your commuting time remembering successful projects in which you've been involved. Replay compliments from bosses and co-workers. Think about problems you've solved, people you've helped and ways you've made your department a better place.

The best jobs will go to people with the most skills. Keep learning. For example:

- Take a public speaking class. Even if you're sure that you'll never have to give a talk, you'll have more confidence when interviewing for a job and feel more comfortable about speaking up at meetings.

- A class in business writing can help you draft clear memos and reports.

- Even if you don't plan to surf the Web, learn how to use the Internet so you understand what others are talking about.

- Read one of the "Dummies" series books on a subject that would give you an edge at work.

- Learn another language, one that is widely spoken by your clients or co-workers.

- Stay up-to-date on new business equipment and software, even if you don't expect to use it.

Look for ways to incorporate what you *want* to do into what you *already* do. For example, if you're in human resources but want to become a business writer, offer to write the employee handbook or newsletter.

"Tell everyone what you want to do and someone will want to help you do it."

—W. Clement Stone,
American writer and businessman

Devote an hour or two each day to nonphone-related work.

Determine if any of your tasks are duplicated by someone else. Can they be taken over by the other person?

Look for ways to get the same job done with less effort and time.

Update your "to-do" list every day. Don't risk overlooking an important deadline or waste mental energy trying to *remember* what needs to get done.

What time of the day are you most productive? Try to do challenging jobs during the time of day when you're most alert and do routine jobs when you're slower.

"All that we are is the result of what we have thought."
—Buddha

Have a thorough understanding of your company's pension or profit-sharing plan. Whether you stay at the company for six years or for seven might have a major impact on your retirement funds!

Understand and observe the requirements and limitations of your company's health insurance program. Bills can add up quickly, and if you haven't followed procedures, the insurance company may refuse to pay.

Develop a network before you need it. Most (80 percent or more) of all nonentry level jobs are not advertised; they're landed through networking. Here are some ways to connect with others and add job skills at the same time:

- Join a service organization. You'll be making a valuable contribution to the community while establishing your contacts.

- Join Toastmasters International to improve your speaking skills. Besides learning to be more comfortable sharing your ideas, you can find job leads through other members, who come from all areas of the community.

- Go to professional meetings alone. You're more likely to make new contacts if you're not spending the time huddled up with associates.

- Get involved in a fund raiser. The skills you develop organizing volunteer workers, planning events, managing a budget and bringing in revenues are directly transferable to your job. You'll also meet people you might never have connected with otherwise.

- Don't hesitate to talk about your accomplishments to your networking contacts. They need to know about your skills and achievements if they're going to help you take advantage of new opportunities.

- Get involved in a project at work that puts you in touch with people from other departments. You make new contacts and they learn your skills; in a shaky corporate environment, you can use all the allies you can get.

Women, leave your role of mother or daughter at home. Attempting to "take care" of co-workers or expecting them to take care of you can detract from your image as a capable businessperson.

Men, leave your role of father or bachelor "catch" at home. Workers who are encouraged to be responsible and are treated with respect will support you in accomplishing your goals at work.

Life is *not* a cabaret. It's an improv.
Forget about scripts. Forget about trying
to have each scene make sense. Forget
about struggling to make your life perfect
and keep it that way. Do your best with
whatever comes up. Be flexible.
Don't take it all so seriously...

Bosses appreciate and sometimes even reward employees who are positive and cooperative when policies and procedures change.

Resisting change is like trying to play baseball while clutching the football from the previous game.

If you resist change, ask yourself why. Are you uncomfortable with uncertainty? Do you fear losing power, freedom, your feeling of competency? Are you concerned the new way may be more work? Cost more money? Be less efficient? Does your ego say what you've established can't be improved?

Some ways to stop resisting change:

- If you're afraid that change means losing power, look for ways to increase your knowledge and your contributions at work.
- If you fear losing your sense of competency, think of all the things you know how to do that you once didn't. Learn to act confident even when you aren't.
- If you're concerned the new way of doing things may cost more money or be less efficient, first determine if it's part of your job to be concerned about such issues. If it is, express your concerns and ask if others have those concerns, too. If they don't, ask what they know that will help you understand and be more comfortable.

Small ways to practice being comfortable with change:

- Go to work by a different route.
- Eat and drink something different at lunch. Sit in a new place at lunch and at staff meetings.
- If you normally talk more than others, take a few days to listen more, and vice versa.
- Buy clothing that's not your usual style.
- Wear your hair in a different style.
- Look for an advantage of doing something the new way. Keep looking until you find at least one.

"Nothing is permanent but change."
—Heraclitus, Greek philosopher

Others who appear smarter may just be better actors

Ask for the help you need to do your job well. For example:

- If you need coaching to be more successful in sales, ask your manager to role-play a sales call with you.
- If you need help prioritizing your work, ask your supervisor for suggestions.
- Ask for more responsibility to make decisions if that would help you offer better service to customers.

- If you've inherited the responsibilities of someone whose job was cut, ask if you can meet with the exiting employee for training. Ask that person's supervisor for recommendations on how to do the job more efficiently.
- From time to time ask your supervisor for feedback on how you're doing and what you could improve.

When faced with an unpleasant task, promise yourself a treat (a cup of coffee, a walk down the hall or a snack) once it's completed.

Search until you find the hidden rules of your job—
the rules that nobody tells you about but that may have
the biggest impact on how your boss judges your
performance. How can you find out what they are?
Watch people who are successful in your company or
department, or ask. Once you discover these rules, follow
them—but keep looking. They can change. They
include:

- Friendship between employees and management
  is/is not appropriate.

- Independent action and decision-making is/is not
  appreciated.

- Your boss does/does not like being involved in
  minor decisions.

- Suggestions to your boss can be made spontaneously/ should be held for an appropriate time.
- Suggestions should be presented verbally/in writing.
- Your boss is/is not comfortable with having you add information during a conversation with others.
- Your boss is more comfortable with a few minutes of social chat before getting to business/would rather jump straight to business matters.

Invest in voice mail instead of call waiting for your home-office phone. When you interrupt one call to answer another, you give the first caller the message that anyone— even a potential wrong number—is more important.

Ways to make your boss happy:

- Be pleasant and cooperative.
- Proofread the work you give her, especially if it will be passed on to others or if it's a rush.
- Don't discuss your boss's faults with co-workers.
- Don't argue with your boss where others can hear.
- Pass along information about competitors or about anything that offers solutions to the challenges of your department or company, with the note "FYI."
- If your boss appears unusually rushed during a project, ask if you can help.
- Consider your boss's opinions or requests politely.
- Remember: If your boss thinks something is important, it is.

Be optimistic. Expect that your job will be there for you for as long as you want it but always have an up-to-date resume and a plan B.

Surround yourself with people who are positive thinkers.

Do work that will bring you positive recognition before you do work that's merely routine or easy.

A new boss wants to sort out the willing helpers from the dead wood. Volunteer for assignments that are important to your boss and ones that play to your strengths.

Listen to what you tell others about your job. If it's negative, look for ways to change the negative parts—or at least your attitude about them.

If you feel underappreciated at work, volunteer your skills away from work and enjoy feeling appreciated.

Slow down. Take your coffee breaks. Life isn't about making lists and seeing how fast you can get everything done, even at work. In case you hadn't noticed, once you finish a list there's another list that's just as urgent.

Don't stay in a job that forces you to do or be anything you're not comfortable doing or being.

Value yourself more for who you are than for what you do.

If you'd like to advance, you may need to find ways to help your boss learn to trust you with more authority

- Win his confidence by being responsible and positive, meeting deadlines and keeping him informed of your progress.
- Tell him why it makes sense for you to be in charge of certain decisions.
- Tell him how your having more authority in one particular area will save time and/or money.
- Suggest that you try the new arrangement for one month, then look at the results.
- Let your boss share the credit for a project's success even if all he did was get out of your way.

If you're assigned to a team and you do most of the work, keep your boss aware of your efforts by sending regular updates. Keep them handwritten and casual. Include others' contributions if you feel uncomfortable with a list about you alone.

Here's how to make time for work you've inherited as a result of downsizing:

- Cancel subscriptions to professional publications that are no longer helpful to you.
- Ask to be taken off routing lists for memos from departments that have nothing to do with your work.

- Question the necessity of every task you do. Stop doing tasks that don't need to be done.
- If someone continually suggests gathering five or six people together for a meeting, see whether just the two of you sitting down for 10 minutes would be sufficient.

"Remember, happiness doesn't depend on who you are or what you have, it depends solely upon what you think."

—Dale Carnegie,
American writer and
educator, 1888-1955

Truth and integrity mean different things to people. Don't let others make you feel unreasonable for your high standards. If you're not comfortable playing a joke on a co-worker, simply say you're not comfortable and decline to be involved. If you don't want to listen to gossip about a co-worker, find a comfortable way to escape or change the subject. If you'd rather go home to your family or just be alone than go out after work with the gang, just say, "Not this time, I have other plans," and don't be forced to reveal your plans if you don't want to.

Put pictures of your family, dog or cat on your desk. They help you remember there is life beyond work.

Be flexible. There may be many ways to accomplish a project. Some may seem better than others, but if your boss wants it done a certain way, be willing to do it that way.

Unfortunately, some bosses aren't very skilled at the job of being a leader. Here are some tips to protect yourself from a difficult boss:

- Be polite, even if your boss isn't.
- Don't be drawn into gripe sessions with other employees.
- If your boss asks for changes and then forgets, document requests and the date.

- Ask yourself what you could do to make situations less difficult. Do it, even if you think you shouldn't have to.
- Document any conversations or activities your boss could use against you.

It's hard to change a rude, insensitive, abusive boss, but it has happened. Before you quit, consider these options:

- Use "I" sentences when you talk to your boss about words or behavior that make you uncomfortable.
- Investigate the possibility of working at home.

- Change your relationship with your boss by changing your attitude. Be patient but firm when demands are unreasonable. Acknowledge positive behavior. Don't take bad behavior personally.
- File a complaint with the human resources or employee services department (useful only if the abuse violates the law).
- Transfer to another department.

Don't wait to be told to do things you already know need to be done.

Have only one project on your desk at a time. Put everything else someplace else. With only one task visible, you won't feel distracted or overwhelmed, and when you finish, you'll have a sense of completion.

Don't put off doing tasks you dread. The dread will cloud your day and your decisions about other things.

Save yourself confusion by dating all documents and drafts.

Don't tease co-workers. Humor that makes anyone uncomfortable isn't humor.

Act on those urges to do something nice for your co-workers: Give a compliment, send a card, distribute a funny cartoon.

When you go to your boss with a problem, have a couple of solutions to offer, too.

Everyone is in sales. Whether you're trying to convince your boss to support a worthy project or a prospective buyer to buy, here are some subtle (and honest) ways to influence someone else:

- Subtly mirror the person's body language.
- Match your breathing with the other person's.
- Adapt the tone of your voice and the speed of your talk to the other person's.
- Use the sensory words (hear, see, feel) they use.
- Match your communication style to theirs—bottom line (brief and to the point), social (concerned about the person as well as the information) or chatty (warm-up conversation before getting to the point).

Be curious. Even if you're sure you know what customers or co-workers have to say, listen. They could surprise you!

"Circumstances do not make a man, they reveal him."
—James Allen, 19th-century writer

If you only talk to your boss when there's trouble, both of you will think trouble when you think of each other.

Don't assume your boss has your best interests in mind, unless they are in line with hers.

Don't expect to be able to do two people's jobs without eliminating half the tasks.

Do your best at work and then leave. Develop a ritual to represent leaving your job (and thoughts about it) at the door.

At some point you are simply as efficient as you're ever going to be. And that's probably okay.

> **It's easy to get so caught up doing the tasks of our jobs that we forget about other things that affect our success. Pay attention to people who are successful in your department, your company...**

Appearance isn't everything, but it certainly counts. Right or wrong, people judge you by what you wear, the way you talk and what you talk about. And they judge fast! To avoid judgments that could block your success:

- Dress in the same style as the successful people in your company.
- Adopt a hairstyle that you can keep neat.
- Wear makeup conservatively.

- Have clean fingernails and repair chipped polish.
- Replace or repair rundown heels and scuffed or soiled shoes, handbags and briefcases.
- Avoid jewelry that makes noise. The rule for jewelry at work? Less is best.
- Understand the messages of color. If you're large, wearing black can make you seem imposing. Brown is sometimes considered old-fashioned. Red makes you appear wild. Blue makes you seem safe.
- Develop a few subjects you can talk to strangers about. Avoid controversial or negative subjects.
- Develop a pleasant voice and a firm handshake, and look people in the eyes.

If your grammar, accent or diction could stand between you and a promotion, fix it. If you're not sure if it could, ask your boss and make it comfortable for him to give an honest answer.

The way you say something can affect your boss's opinion of you. "What should I do with this?" sounds like you don't know your job and you have no initiative. "What do you think I should do?" indicates you value your boss' opinion. "I think the best thing to do with this would be... What do you think?" shows you have a plan but are willing to let your boss have input.

Keep up-to-date on the language style your company prefers. If your company doesn't have an obvious style, you are generally safe adopting the language about age, gender and race that a conservative magazine or newspaper uses.

Ways to communicate better:

- Know what the key message is and state it clearly.
- Write the way you talk.
- Use contractions.
- Use the simplest word or phrase: "use" instead of "usage," "because" instead of "in view of the fact that" and "here is" instead of "please find enclosed."

A new boss may have a new communication style. Take your cues from the way she talks to you. All business, to the point? Warm, open? Talk to her in the same way.

If you're not sure how long a job will take, get input from your boss. People tend to underestimate the length of time it will take them to do something but overestimate the length of time someone else will need to do the job.

No matter how busy you are, don't let your customers feel like they're interrupting you.

Don't make your boss prove he or she has more power than you.

Sometimes shortcuts aren't. Don't rely on spell-check; you could miss words that are spelled correctly but are used incorrectly or in the wrong place. You could miss catching sentences that repeat information and sentences that aren't complete.

If you can't explain your idea to your boss in 30 seconds you're not ready to explain it.

"Simplify, simplify."

—Henry David Thoreau,
19th-century American writer
and philosopher

How to recognize when communication breaks down:

• Someone appears to listen but doesn't look at
  you or doesn't respond.
• Someone responds with an unenthusiastic "yes,"
  "no," "ummm" or "okay."
• Someone leaves you voice mail and notes but
  avoids talking to you in person.

If you work at home, have a separate phone line installed and answer as if you were in an office, even if your desk is in a corner of the bedroom. Close the door before making or taking calls in order to eliminate the sounds of children or barking dogs.

Take charge of your career: If you're passed over for advancement, make an opportunity to meet with your manager to express your goals and ask what you might do to improve your chances for promotion.

If you don't work the traditional work schedule, post your hours at your workstation so others won't be frustrated trying to find you.

Record voice mail that says when you'll be in and how you can be reached in the meantime. If you work part-time at home, list your phone and fax number.

While it may be important to do things right, it's more important to do the right things.

It isn't pushy to follow your business letter with a phone call. It's smart! How will you know it was received unless you check?

If you're giving a talk, go early to check seating, lighting and sound. Remember, Murphy was an optimist.

If you find your mind wandering during meetings, take notes. It doesn't matter whether you'll read them again; the process will help you pay attention.

Beliefs that get women into trouble:

• Your ideas are not as important as others'.
• Things should be fair.
• It's your job to make everyone feel good.
• If you ask for what you need you're being pushy.
• Everyone should like you.

Beliefs that get men into trouble:

• You have to prove yourself constantly.
• You're doing more than the next person.
• Work rules don't apply to you.
• Women aren't as competent as men are.
• Everyone should like you.

Often the best way to handle an office backstabber is face-to-face. Without being emotional, say something like, "I've heard you don't think my project suggestions are any good. I'd like to know what's on your mind. Can you tell me more?" You probably won't learn anything helpful, but you do put the backstabber on notice that you know.

If you work at home, stay in touch with your manager. Even though it feels like you're being parented, check in to let him know what's going on. Let your boss know how often you check your e-mail and at what times so he will know when to expect a reply. You want him to value your work and have confidence that you will get the job done.

Before you host a business lunch or dinner, visit the restaurant and introduce yourself to the maitre d'. Ask for reserved seating in a good area. Ask if you can prearrange a 15 to 20 percent tip so all that's required on the big day is your signature. Taking care of details beforehand makes you appear very smooth and in charge.

Check your company's policy before sending or accepting gifts from business associates outside your company.

When your boss wants you to drop everything to do something else and you can't because of a conflicting deadline:

- Acknowledge that her request is important.
- Make it clear that your current schedule can't accommodate the new task.
- Suggest someone else who might be able to do the new task, and be willing to help arrange that.
- Agree to do what you boss asks if the alternative doesn't work and if the deadline on your current project can be extended.
- Show with your voice, words and body language that your goal is to be helpful.

Don't put all your job skills in one basket. Always be aware of what other companies in your field are doing by getting to know a few people who work for your major competitors and reading your industry's trade magazines.

Have a few disinterested confidants to go to for advice.

Recognize the symptoms of job burnout while you can still turn it around:

- You're bored.

- You put off starting a task until the last minute.

- You get angry easily with yourself and others.

- You notice others' attitudes changing toward you.

- You dread going to work.

- You look for excuses to miss work.

Burnout is serious, but not fatal. To get through it:

- Forget about work when you're away from the office.

- Look for ways to make your job more interesting.

- See if you can trade some job responsibilities with a co-worker.

- If you've got vacation time coming, use it.

- Take classes that could lead you to a new job.

"There is more to life than increasing its speed."
—Mahatma Gandhi

Few people can know it all. But if you hang out with people who are successful in your field, you'll hear them talk about the more important information. Make sure you know the same things. Ask them where they go for information. Read the popular business books. Know the current thinking on topics such as conflict, change, ethics, business economics, negotiation and dealing with difficult people.

Don't be too open about all the things you don't know. It's okay to hedge when someone tries to pin you down. Just find a way to update yourself quickly.

People in authority like you to recognize their authority. When you do, it opens the door for them to graciously say yes to you.

When you really want information, ask open-ended questions rather than closed-ended ones. For example: "How do you find the Internet helpful?" instead of "Do you like the Internet?"

Take a lesson from Charles and Di: Don't say anything on a cellular phone you wouldn't want to be repeated on the evening news.

Ditto for e-mail. Even when you delete workplace e-mail, it may linger on your company's backup tapes. E-mail has been admitted as evidence in some legal actions, and some companies review tapes for possibly embarrassing communications.

Consider sending a memo by e-mail and the files (especially long ones) by regular mail.

More e-mail etiquette:

- Don't leave the sender guessing about whether you received the message.
- Avoid humor that could be misunderstood.
- Don't be lulled by e-mail's informality. If you're writing to a business colleague, don't be formal but do be businesslike.
- Reread your e-mail and spell-check it before you push the send button.
- Don't send e-mail in ALL CAPS. It can be hard to read.
- Work out problems in person, not on e-mail.
- Protect your password.

Leave brief voice mail messages that ask to be called back if there's more to discuss. People get impatient listening to a string of messages. If yours is long, it may not get the attention it deserves.

If you fax vital information, call to confirm that it arrived. Faxes, like socks in the laundry, can disappear. They can miss the collection tray and land in a pile on the floor. Number pages of faxed material, even if just by hand. It makes identifying missing pages easier.

Sending confidential or personal information via fax is like putting a confidential message in *The New York Times*.

If you're a manager challenged with accomplishing your goals with more work and fewer employees, consider these ways to motivate your overburdened staff:

- Look for ways to make employees glad they work for you. Help your company find ways to make all employees glad they work for your company.
- Don't expect your employees to do extra work for free. If you want them to suggest customer service opportunities or marketing ideas, offer a reward.

- Don't just tell employees what they're going to do. Ask for input.
- Look for ways to motivate employees, not control them.
- Determine what's important to each employee and create incentives based on that. Encourage employees to take ownership of their projects. Be clear about why a project is important. When target goals aren't met, encourage employees to find solutions. Give employees the credit they deserve for a job well done.
- When you communicate change, tell employees why. They'll make up a reason if you don't, so telling them the truth will save everybody time and, maybe, worry.

- Employees won't do it your way if they don't think it will work. Sell them on why it will, or invite them to come up with a better plan.
- Don't frustrate employees by expecting them to do what *you* would do if you were doing their job.

The best time to find a new job is before you leave your old one.

Career specialists tell us most people today
change jobs—even careers!—five to seven times
in their lives. Sometimes it's by choice, sometimes
it isn't. Knowing where to look for a job has
never been more important. Interviewing has
become a science. Learning to read the signs
that it's time to look for a new job is essential...

It's naive to assume you'll have your job for as long
as you want it—even if you're great at it or are the boss's

favorite. Be alert for these clues that your job may be in jeopardy:

- You didn't get your routine raise.

- Your company is experiencing serious financial woes.

- Your primary projects are eliminated and aren't replaced with others.

- There is widespread talk of "restructuring" your department and "reclassifying" the positions.

- Your boss is fired or leaves and isn't replaced.

- Another company buys your company, and it already has people who do what you do.

Signs that it might be time to look for a new job:

- You're experiencing anxiety, headaches, backaches, ulcers and depression frequently.
- You're bored at work most of the time.
- You've reached the top of your salary range.
- You feel you aren't making the contribution you want to make.
- You're working under your potential, and there are no possibilities to grow.
- Your job is keeping you so busy it's preventing you from pursuing your career.

Before you leave a job, for any reason, be clear about why you're leaving. Avoid getting into a new job with the same conditions.

If you want a specific letter of recommendation, ask your boss if you can write it yourself and have him sign it.

Your cover letter is as important as your resume. Get a book on how to write resumes and cover letters and make yours professional and easy to read.

Don't send the same resume and cover letter to every potential employer. Change key words to reflect qualities requested in the ad or important to the company's business.

If you have the option of faxing or mailing your resume, mail it. The quality of the paper and typeface makes a better impression. Hand-deliver it if time is a concern. If you must fax it, print a copy on white paper and make sure the typeface will reproduce clearly.

If you post your resume online, describe your experience with nouns employers can find in word searches. Remember, using your full name at the top of your resume may reveal to others at your company that you're looking.

Good books for job/career seekers:

- *What Color is Your Parachute?* by Richard Nelson Bolles.
- *I Could Do Anything If I Only Knew What It Was* by Barbara Sher with Barbara Smith.
- *Real Magic* by Wayne Dyer.
- *The Art of Managing People* by Phillip L. Hunsaker and Anthony J. Alessandra.

If you're looking for a job, do something toward getting one every day.

Check out electronic classified ads, career counseling and company profiles on the Internet and other online services.

Take advantage of your city or county's free job counseling service.

Have a friend question you in a mock interview.

Bring an extra resume to an interview. Tuck it into a leather or leather-look folder along with a pad of paper for taking notes.

Try to schedule one or two interviews for jobs you don't care about as practice for interviewing for jobs you want.

Think of an employment interview as a job. That job is to convince the interviewer that you want the position and that you're the best candidate—even if you're not sure that you do or you are. The time to decide is after you've left the final interview.

Go on an interview with the idea that you're interviewing them rather than the other way around. You are, and it will make you feel more relaxed.

When an interviewer says, "Tell me about a time when you...":

- Discuss a situation where you were successful solving a problem.
- Use a situation that somehow relates to the company where you're applying.
- Don't give a blow-by-blow description of the event—just enough details to convey what happened, how you responded and why, and what the results were.
- Explain how past experience or training led you to make the decision you did.
- Tell how your way of handling the situation contributed to the company's finances, employee morale, customer service or departmental goals.

Things you should discover when interviewing for a job:

- The qualities the boss would like you to have.

- The boss's preferred management style.

- Why the former employee left.

- How your job performance will be evaluated.

- The average length of employment for people in this department.

- The major tasks you'll be asked to do.

While you're waiting for your job interview, be friendly with the secretary or administrative assistant. Briefly chat with him or her. More than half of 150 hiring executives who were asked said they considered their assistant's opinions of a candidate important.

Some questions to ask a potential boss:

• "How do you decide if an employee is doing a good job or not? Is it over a period of time? Is it after a certain number of events?"
• "How is success rewarded?"

- "What made you decide to work for the company?"

- "What is the general work atmosphere in the company and department?"

- "How has downsizing affected the company's or department's workload and morale? Is more downsizing expected?"

- "How do you see my experience as fitting with what you need?"

- "What is the next step? When will you be making a decision?"

During an interview, pay attention to how you feel about the person who will be your boss. The job description may sound wonderful, but if your boss is rude, impatient, insensitive, uncertain, unclear or unethical, your dream job could be a nightmare.

Practice friendly body language—smiling, nodding your head, leaning forward slightly when you talk—at home in front of a mirror so it will look natural during an interview.

Be prepared for these tricky questions an interviewer might ask:

- "Describe the last disagreement you had with a boss."
- "How would you deal with a client who (fill in your worst nightmare)?"
- "What would you do if the company asked you to move to another location?"

During the interview, avoid crossing your arms or allowing your facial expressions to show boredom, impatience or disgust. Make eye contact but don't stare the interviewer down.

Before an interview, practice an answer to "Where do you see yourself in five years?" Research the company: Do they expect employees to find a job and do it for life? Are they eager to hire employees who want to advance?

Plan an answer to an interview question about your weak points. Choose something that can also be considered a strength. Be prepared to give an example.

Even though the majority of employees leave a company because of personality conflicts, an employment interviewer won't want to hear that's why you did. It's his or her goal to hire someone with excellent skills—on the job *and* with people.

If the interviewer points out that you don't have any experience in the industry you're trying to enter, ask what the most important aspects of the job are. Then describe how you were successful in those areas in your previous industry.

Read the business section of the paper. Know if a potential employer has been in the news.

Find something in the interviewer's office to relate to and comment positively on it.

If a job interviewer presses you for details about an employer and you can't think of anything good to say, focus on the valuable experiences you had there, on skills you learned, on areas of growth.

Fears of prospective employers (that you can help them overcome):

- You won't be able to do the job.

- You won't be willing to work as diligently as needed.

- You will ignore the boss's requests and instructions.

- You will make your boss look bad.

- You won't get along with the other workers.

Ways to evaluate a company's proemployee policy:

- Are there equivalent salaries for men and women?
- What is the ratio of men to women in middle and upper management?
- Does the company offer flexible hours?
- Is personal time available for taking care of children and elderly parents?
- What is the policy on maternity leave?
- How comprehensive are the medical benefits?
- What are the opportunities for advancement?
- Does the company promote from within?
- What is the vacation policy?
- Is there a profit-sharing/401(k) plan?

It's management's job to offer you a salary that is beneficial to the company's financial picture, not necessarily a salary that reflects your worth. Here are several strategies for success in negotiation salary:

- Know approximately what you want and the absolute least you would accept.
- Know what other employers are paying for the work you'll be doing.
- Never get into an adversarial position with the salary negotiator. Your goal is to be so appealing that the company is willing to give you what you want even if that's more than it planned to spend.

- Avoid naming a figure. Instead ask, "What is the salary range for this position?"

- If the figure is too low, say, "I really like the job and know I would make some valuable contributions, but the minimum I could accept is (fill in the blank)." If that sounds too pushy for you, say, "I'd feel more comfortable with...". The figure should be a little higher than your true minimum. Then say earnestly, "I know the contributions I'll make will be well worth it to the XYZ company."

- If negotiations stall, ask to think about the offer for 24 hours.

- Make a list of the positives and negatives of the job and weigh them against the dollar value. You might surprise yourself by deciding the money is less important than some of the other benefits.

- If you call back to accept a low offer, try to get an earlier performance appraisal/raise date than normal, health insurance effective immediately, a longer vacation or some other concession.

A promotion is a new job. In the era of downsizing, it can mean a lot of extra work and responsibility. Know what it will entail before you accept it or turn it down.

Here are some questions to ask yourself or the person making the offer:

- Was it offered to others? If it was turned down, why?

- Is it a true promotion or a lateral move?

- What is the new salary?

- Is there training available?

- Will the new job demand more time than you're willing to give?

- Will you have the authority to accomplish what you've been charged to do?

- Will co-workers resent it if you accept?
- Is it a dead-end job? A job that could easily be eliminated?

Questions to ask before you agree to telecommute:

- How will you motivate yourself?
- How will your performance be evaluated?
- Will you be overlooked for promotions (and do you care)?
- Will you be able to participate in office competitions?
- Who will keep you in the loop and how?

You may not feel like you're in control of your destiny, but you can learn to be. Practice looking for ways to make your life the way you want it to be...

Life is what happens after you say, "Yes, but...". When someone suggests you look for a job in a field you like better and you say, "Yes, but I probably couldn't get one," you won't. If someone encourages you to go back to school to learn new job skills and you say, "Yes, but I really can't afford it," you'll stay stuck in your old field forever.

*"Don't be afraid to take a big step if one is indicated.
You can't cross a chasm in two small jumps."*

—David Lloyd George,
Welsh liberal statesman, 1863-1945

Identify the messages you learned as a child that stand in the way of your being happy or successful now. Understand how these messages work against you and let them go. Are these familiar?:

- What will other people think?
- Can't you be satisfied with what you have?
- Be careful; stay safe; don't get hurt.
- Don't get your hopes up.
- What makes you think you're so smart?

Most companies have them; some people have them; *everybody* should have them. Companies call them "mission statements." People call them a "purpose." Both mean the same thing: a goal to reach—not in having, but in doing and being. When you know what your purpose is, it's easier to make decisions. You simply ask yourself: Would this help me accomplish my purpose?

Don't blame others when something goes wrong. Don't blame yourself endlessly, either. Just find ways to do it differently next time.

Read and understand your employee handbook. Consider it your company's contract with you. When you accept the handbook, the company may legally consider that you have accepted its policies about insurance plans, retirement benefits, dress codes, holiday and sick-leave pay and dozens of other issues. Employees who don't read the information are still bound by company policies.

"We fill up our space with things that put us just this side of doing our dreams."

—Bill Sparkman,
corporate trainer

More ways to reduce stress at work:

- Don't try to control the uncontrollable. If you've tried your best to change something and continually met resistance, give up. At least for a while.
- Determine a quitting time and stick to it. Don't stay at work until everything is done.
- Learn to stop working on a project when it's time to eat, take a break or go home.

Begin slowly to make the changes you want to make in yourself, but begin now.

Ask yourself frequently:

- What do I really want? What's the story I tell myself about why I don't have it?
- What do I want to get rid of? What's the story I tell myself about why I still have it?
- What thoughts and behaviors have brought me here?
- What thoughts and behaviors do I need to change to take me someplace else?

When you plan a new behavior, also plan what you'll do when you find yourself reverting to the old way.

It's not remarkable to keep trying after two or three failures. What's remarkable is to keep trying until you succeed.

When your boss and co-workers make you mad, they control you in ways you'd never let them if they asked. Instead of letting what they say or do trigger angry feelings, practice pretending you're on stage. See them as actors repeating lines that may or may not be true. Practice responding without taking what they say or do personally.

"In the end, the only people who fail are those who do not try."
>—David Viscott,
>American writer and psychiatrist

You are your own fortune teller. Every word you say helps create your future.

"We cannot direct the wind but we can adjust the sails."
>—Anonymous

Eight phrases to retire:

- "If only..."

- "Yes, but..."

- "Someday..."

- "I'll try..."

- "I can't..."

- "I would if..."

- "Maybe later..."

- "I shudda, wudda, cudda..."

People never used to give much thought to taking care of themselves. Men worked to earn money to take care of their families. Women worked at home to take care of their families. Under ideal circumstances, everyone was taken care of by someone else. Under less-than-ideal circumstances, there was a fair amount of bitterness, resentment, anger and frustration. Today the roles are less rigid, and we're learning we're happier when we take care of ourselves.

Is it more important to you to work 16 hours a day and earn a zillion dollars or is it more important to work eight hours and have time for yourself, your family and friends?

Make work fun. Celebrate birthdays and work anniversaries. Celebrate traditions of co-workers from other countries. Post a humorous Far Side cartoon on a blank piece of paper. Delete the caption and invite co-workers to fill in captions of their own. Have a picture, a figure or a coffee mug on your desk that reminds you of something funny or fun.

"The important thing is this: to be able at any moment to sacrifice what we are for what we could become."

—Charles Du Bos,
French critic, 1882-1939

Leave work at work. Do something on the way home to change gears. Listen to a tape of your favorite music. Stop and browse at a favorite store, stop at a favorite park, meditate. Make notes about things in your life you're thankful for.

Don't listen to other people's tales of woe endlessly. Trust yourself to know what's best for you. Turn down the volume on messages that come from others.

Prescriptions for when you're stressed:

- Notice if you're holding your breath. Breathe.
- Notice where your shoulders are. If they're up around your neck, relax them.
- Notice the muscles in your stomach. If they're tight, relax them.
- Take three slow, deep breaths.
- Ask yourself if the situation is life-threatening or if it's your responses that might be.
- Give yourself permission not to be perfect.
- Concentrate on doing your best instead of doing better than everybody else.

Turn down stress by turning off the news and rage DJs on your way to work. Instead:

- Play a motivation tape.

- Play a how-to tape.

- Play a tape you made of work facts you want to remember.

- Play soothing music until the last five minutes before you arrive at work. Play energizing music the last five minutes.

- Play a comedy tape and laugh a little.

- Think about something fun you plan to do.

Note to the workaholic: Just because you can check voice mail and e-mail at 11:30 p.m. doesn't mean you should.

Treat yourself to a massage once a month.

Pay attention to what your body is trying to tell you. Constant headaches and backaches can warn that you're under too much stress. Don't just accept the fact that you are; find ways to decrease or eliminate it.

Life is not a challenge for you to attempt to get more work done than anybody else.

Recapture the child you were when:

- You knew you could succeed at anything.
- You knew you were the most important person in your life.
- You asked for what you wanted instead of what you thought you should.
- You said what you felt instead of what you thought others wanted to hear.

Do things on the weekends that are different from what you do at work. If your work is intense or competitive, do something restful. If you play sports, don't play ones where you keep score.

Work habits that keep you stressed:

- Missing stretch breaks.
- Drinking coffee all day.
- Not delegating/not asking for help.

Your mind creates stress, not your life.

*"No one on his deathbed has ever said,
'I wish I'd spent more time at the office.'"*

—Anonymous

The highest incidence of heart attacks is on Monday at 9 a.m. Plan something pleasant for all your Monday mornings.

More ways to reduce stress at work:

- When you have the urge to yawn or sigh, do it.

- Take a short break every few hours and find someplace private to stretch.

Don't expect more of yourself than you can possibly deliver, even if your boss does.

Safety can be hazardous to your health—if you stay at a "safe" job that is making you ill.

Listen to motivational and self-improvement tapes in your car on the way to work.

Stop struggling. If it's you against the world, the world is probably going to win.

Who you are is more important than what you do. Don't feel bad about a job you enjoy that doesn't fit into others' visions of what you should do.

Look for ways you sabotage your own success. Where did you get the idea that success is bad? Dangerous? That you're not good enough? That it costs more than it's worth?